Lost Souls
of the
Lost Township

Untold Life Stories
of the People Buried
in the *Davis-Smith Cemetery*
Kansas City, Jackson County, Missouri

Paul R. Petersen & David W. Jackson

The Orderly Pack Rat
Kansas City, Missouri
2011

Petersen, Paul R. (1949-) and David W. Jackson (1969-)
    Lost Souls of the Lost Township: Untold Life Stories of the People Buried in the *Davis-Smith Cemetery*, Kansas City, Jackson County, Missouri.
    76 p.   cm.
    Includes bibliographical references and index.

    ISBN: 0-9704308-6-8

1. Missouri–Biography. 2. Cemeteries–Preservation. 3. Cemeteries–Missouri–Kansas City. 4. Davis-Smith Cemetery (Kansas City, Mo.)–History. 5. Jackson County (Mo.) Genealogy. 6. Cultural Property–Protection–Missouri–Kansas City. I. Petersen, Paul R. (1949-). II. David W. Jackson (1969-). III. Title.

Published by:
The Orderly Pack Rat
Kansas City, Missouri
david.jackson@orderlypackrat.com
www.orderlypackrat.com

Remember friends, as you pass by,

As you are now, so once was I.

As I am now, so you shall be,

Prepare for death and follow me.

Epitaph of
Sarah "Sally" Ann (Davis) Landers
buried in Davis-Smith Cemetery

TABLE OF CONTENTS

FOREWORD

For at least the last 25 years, an untold number of people have sought the best way to preserve the *Davis-Smith Cemetery*, where members of the pioneer John Davis and Reuben Marshall Harris, Sr., families...and other intermarrying families...are interred.

That one of Jackson County's handful of Revolutionary War veterans is buried in the *Davis-Smith Cemetery* is unique in and of itself. But, wait, there's more. Much more. Imagine the lives of those souls buried in this pioneer graveyard...and the long-forgotten life stories that tell of a time when our own neighborhood was a wilderness opening onto vast, virgin prairies.

Recently, the book by Paul R. Petersen, *Quantrill of Missouri: The Making of a Guerilla Warrior: The Man, the Myth, the Soldier*, revealed a wealth of stories that were consistently well-recorded and referenced, making the lives of the people buried in the *Davis-Smith Cemetery* come to life. It can no longer be viewed as just a vacant ¼ acre of land without life, meaning or purpose, but rather, it echoes the voices of persons who lived near there and contributed to our community not so long ago.

Petersen is a lifelong resident of Jackson County, Missouri, and lives in Raytown, very near the *Davis-Smith Cemetery* in Kansas City's eastern, fifth district. Being a combat infantry veteran of three wars, Petersen is uniquely qualified to interpret the nature of guerrilla warfare that characterized the Missouri-Kansas Border War and Civil War era as Jackson Countians experienced. His knowledge of William Clarke Quantrill and his partisan rangers adds to his credibility in relaying factual information about the residents—particularly Southerners—who lived in this community through such difficult times.

Anyone with a remote interest in local history and its preservation should be thankful for Petersen's time and interest in this important project.

This book is organized to focus on the lives (and sometimes tragic deaths) of the people who are buried in the *Davis-Smith Cemetery*. Interspersed, are incidents and events that transpired during their lifetimes, affecting them and those they knew. Additional background information provides readers with a broader picture of the life and times of the people we seek to memorialize.

It is the wish of many (from neighbors, historians and descendants) that this very small, but extremely unique burying ground may be preserved in-tact, marked, and recognized as an historically significant site, and that it be meaningfully incorporated as an *amenity* to modern development that is sure to envelope the surrounding area.

Hopefully, future readers enjoying the history presented in this book will applaud those of us who successfully worked *together* "in-the-now" and in a positive way to provide them the unique opportunity to visit and view a very notable spot in historic Jackson County, Missouri.

With many thanks in advance to those who may make it so....

David W. Jackson
Kansas City, Missouri
Memorial Day, 2011

PREFACE

The information presented here is taken from factual accounts, original documents, and first-hand personal recollections. Foremost is a recollection of the Harris family descendants, Mrs. L. E. Harris and Mrs. M. A. Tucker, of Warsaw, Missouri, who provided to the Kansas City Chapter of the Daughters of the American Revolution (DAR) in 1933 the names and personal information about those whom they remembered having been buried in the *Davis-Smith Cemetery*. The DAR published this information in a publication titled, *Vital Historical Records of Jackson County, Missouri: 1828-1876*, which contains abstracts of Jackson County's early church and pioneer cemetery records roughly covering Jackson County's first 50 years. Testimony of one of the more recent owners of the property, Mrs. Dorothy Hussey, is also invaluable to the recorded history of this parcel.

The DAR listed data about the people buried in the "Smith Cemetery," though the specific name(s) of those bearing the Smith surname could not be recalled in 1933 by the Harris descendants. And, the DAR, apparently, were unable to identify Davis family descendants when compiling their data in 1933. The DAR compilers' likely reasoning for listing this burying ground as the "Smith Cemetery," however, was that it was known that members of the Smith family had married into the Davis family, and it was the Smiths who had consecrated the ¼-acre tract as a burial ground. Both families, then, had owned this land.

It goes without saying that there are certainly any number of relatives, friends and neighbors of the Davis, Smith and Harris families that are buried in this ¼-acre parcel of ground. Without available data, their names may never be known.

Many of these pioneers never had a formal tombstone at the time of burial. In those days, headstones were a luxury not affordable to most. Fieldstones marked many burials in the 19th century. The DAR only discovered one tombstone in 1933 when they performed a site-inspection of this parcel, and published their findings the next year. For others who had been afforded tombstones in the *Davis-Smith Cemetery*, farmers owning the land beyond the 1930s removed the surface stones so that the area could be used as a field for crops, and a hog pen.

Unscrupulous actions from the past are difficult to justify. We recognize more recent landowners for sharing their remembrances and the traditions that had been handed down to them. To the present landowner whose property surrounds the *Davis-Smith Cemetery*, we credit an increased awareness and appreciation for this historic spot, and applaud the positive steps recently taken to better locate and demarcate the ¼-acre parcel in question. The next steps may be to rededicate the Cemetery and erect an historical marker to honor those buried there in order to educate residents and visitors, and to show respect for the Jackson County pioneers resting there, and their descendants.

As you read about the true life stories of those who lived in this area, some of whom are buried in the *Davis-Smith Cemetery*, we hope this publication may tell you something about the lives that these Jackson Countians led, and the times in which they walked on this earth. We hope you, too, might join with others to ensure that the proper thing is done to save and honor this small, sacred spot.

Hidden from visible sight today, some 20,000 cars pass by the *Davis-Smith Cemetery* daily. Situated on a slight rise between State Highway 350 on the eastern boundary of Raytown and the undeveloped area of Kansas City, Missouri, the earthly remains of more than 30 souls resting there go unnoticed and unmarked. The graves have been desecrated and discarded by time and the uncaring hand of progress called modern development. These people lived, loved, married, had children, settled a new territory, tilled the virgin soil, made the area prosperous, achieved success in their vocations, and fought for freedoms during the most turbulent times in our nation's history. Some of these people were buried with the full dignity they deserved, while others during the course of the Civil War were hastily buried in their saddle blankets with only a few close comrades to mourn their passing. What had formerly been erected as lasting tributes by their relatives and friends, their tombstones over the years became weathered, broken, vandalized, or removed. Despite all that has happened since the people who were laid to rest there are still deserving of our respect, and it's up to us to recognize their value to our shared past.

A CRY FOR RECOGNITION

Was it really so long ago? The year was 1821. Missouri had been admitted to the Union as a slave state. From 1788 to 1855 the United States granted military bounty land warrants for military service during wartime. And, there were several wars during that time period, including war to gain our freedom from England and war over territory with France and Spain. Many of our ancestors died so that we live free. This is a statement often espoused . . . Do we truly appreciate it? A land bounty was a grant of land from the Federal government as a reward to repay veterans for the risks and hardships they endured in the service of their country.

Between 1847 and 1855 the United States granted an additional series of increasingly generous land bounties, first to attract enlistments in the Mexican War, then to reward surviving veterans of all wars since 1790, and finally to include those who served in the Revolutionary War. It was not only the Federal government that gave soldiers bounty land as payment for services, but state governments did also. At the time of the Revolutionary War, with no stable Federal government having been established yet, it was the state government land bounties that were most meaningful to soldiers.

Jackson County, Missouri, was formed in 1826. It is an important fact to remember that much of the land had been surveyed from 1817-1826, even before statehood. However, Township 48, Range 32, was considered worthless because the western portion was prairie land with soil too hard to easily plow and the eastern side was a wilderness of trees. According to legend, the reason this area was not surveyed along with the rest of the surrounding countryside was explained as: "A surveyor running the section lines drank too much at a distillery while working, lost his hat and notes, was so ashamed of his loss that he made up the story that there was such a great magnetic force in this area that his compass could not work properly. Other stories were a wild sow destroyed his notes, that it was a goat that prevented him from producing the survey, that it was prairie land and would not pay the government to have the survey," but whatever the reason the area of the Lost Township was not surveyed until 1843.[1]

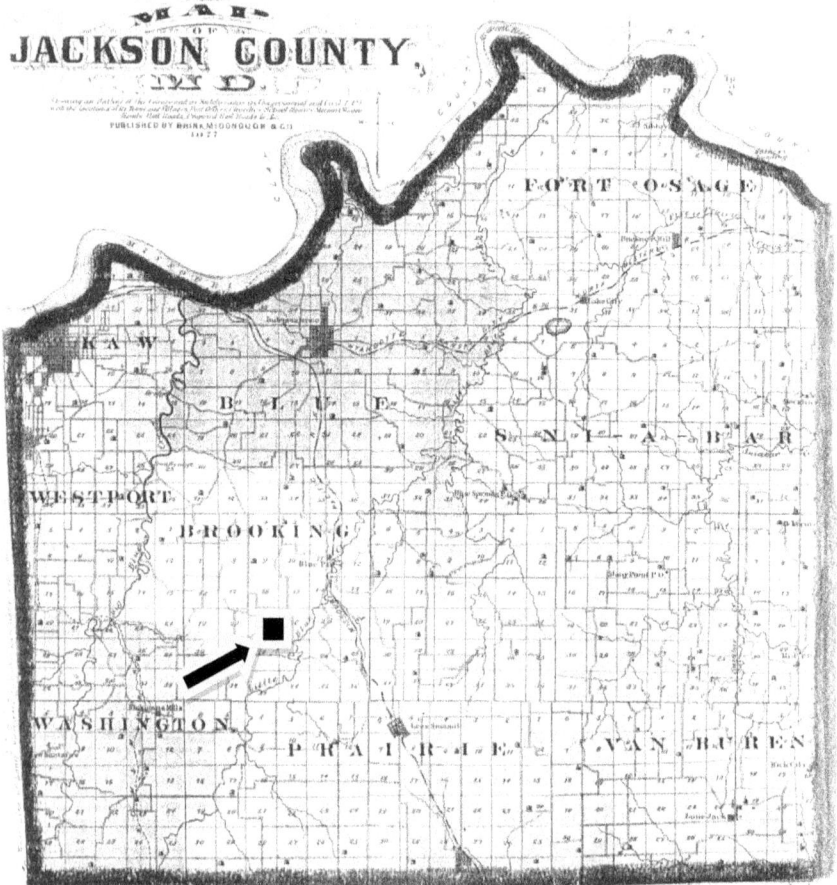

Map from the *Illustrated Historical Atlas of Jackson County, Missouri*, 1877. Arrow and box indicate Section 15, Township 48, Range 32, the location of the *Davis-Smith Cemetery*.

---

[1] Union Historical Company. *History of Jackson County, Missouri*. (Kansas City, Mo.: Birdsall, Williams & Co., 1881), 104.

In the meantime, there were persons living in the area who staked out claims. Settlers began arriving into the un-surveyed, or Lost Township, as early as 1836, spying out land for a place to farm, simply looking for a place to call home. They were allowed to stake out preemptive claims for 160-acres of land on which they would start a farm. By 1844, the Federal government allowed these persons to purchase land for $1.25 an acre; some received a military land grant for service rendered in past wars.

"The early settlements were all in or near the timber or some spring of water, the settlers thinking the prairie land only difficult to be subdued, but actually worthless as agricultural purposes were concerned. When they first began breaking the prairie they used the "barshear" plow, to which they attached four to eight yoke of oxen."[2]

These first settlers had left behind the safety and comfort of the deep South forsaking friends in Kentucky, Tennessee, Virginia and the Carolinas looking for a new life and a new home out West bravely facing the uncertainties of a new environment. The treaty between the United States and the Osage Indians had been finalized in 1825 prompting an expanded growth of settlers. But, as they settled into a new land they brought with them the most important things: they brought their families, a few of their most prized possessions, their Bibles, their faith in God, and their religion.

The settlers living in the surrounding area soon became an extended family as marriages interwove social relationships. Despite the hardships of the times, entertainment relieved the day-to-day pressures of life on the frontier. Some of the more wealthy families owned an organ in their home where friends and neighbors would gather on special occasions to engage in singing and dancing. On evenings and holidays, men and boys gathered together at the home of William and Matilda Muir, and their son, Boone T. Muir, to engage in horse races, foot races, wrestling and shooting matches.

---

[2] Union Historical Company, 103.

It was there in the Lost Township eight miles south of Independence, Missouri, that the *Davis-Smith Cemetery* first came into being. The area had no formal designation other than "lying close to Independence." Farther south it was known as Hickman's Mill. The area had two villages: Raytown and Little Blue. The town of Little Blue was located in the valley while Raytown was centrally situated on a higher plateau called the Blue Prairie, the ridge between the Big and Little Blue Rivers. The Lost Township was re-named the Brooking Township when Brooking was established in 1872, and addresses were often given as "Independence," the nearest town of any size or import.

The south-facing, Lexington Avenue, front façade of the 1838 Jackson County Courthouse on Independence Square, ca. 1850.

Mr. and Mrs. Lewis Starr

One of the earliest settlers to migrate to the Lost Township was Lewis Starr, a Revolutionary War veteran lured from Grayson County, Virginia, to the bountiful section south of Independence, Missouri. Like many of his compatriots, settlers to this area were mainly from the upper South, the majority coming from Virginia, first settling in Kentucky before continuing on to Missouri where the prospect of good farm land and a chance to make a new beginning seemed most appealing. Starr was listed in the census as a farmer, but he also ran a saw mill and grist mill.

Most early settlers initially built a log cabin with an average size around 15 by 16 feet. They also needed a smoke house and corn crib. Starr's gristmill over the Little Blue River was one of the most important buildings of the community before he sold it, along with five acres, to Briscoe Davis and Calvin Landers. His neighbors were dependent on the local mill as bread was a staple part of the diet. Starr's mill had many different uses. One of them was for grinding grains such as wheat, rye, oats, or barley into a better grade of flour and meal. Early mills were almost always built and supported by farming communities and Starr received for his service the "miller's toll" in lieu of wages.

In Jackson County, there was an abundance of fresh springs. The Little Blue River coursed its way through the valley of the Little Blue which ran parallel to the "Independence - Harrisonville Road" on the east (Lee's Summit Road today). A telegraph line ran along the roadway between the two towns, and the road also served to connect the stage lines, which brought the local news from as far away as St. Louis. The surrounding terrain was wild, but some cultivation had begun in the bottomland.

Though Starr's land lay partly in the valley of the Little Blue, the river bottoms were covered with trees of every variety. All the valleys were broken and densely wooded. The gently rolling prairies were carpeted with luxuriant grasses and surrounded by thick belts of timber. The timbered hollows and ravines were covered with thicket almost as dense as a Mexican chaparral.

It was there that Starr settled with his family, near a neighbor, William Moore, *another* Revolutionary War veteran, whose home still survives as a private residence today.

Starr's family included his wife, six sons; Christopher, John J., Joseph, Monroe, William Henderson & Jeremiah and three daughters, Anna "Annie," Matilda, and Mary "Polly" Ann. Beginning in 1844, the Starr family claimed over 300 acres between them settling in the Lost Township of Jackson County.

Log cabin of Revolutionary War veteran, William Moore, in the valley of the Little Blue, typical of an 1820s home likely resembling that of fellow compatriot, Lewis Starr.

Lewis Starr died around January 17, 1848. His wife died before 1849. An outbreak of cholera was sweeping the United States at that time. It took the life of former U. S. President James K. Polk. Cholera, believed spread from ships from England, pervaded the Mississippi River system, killing over 4,500 in St. Louis, and over

3,000 in New Orleans, as well as thousands in New York. Cholera also spread along the California, Santa Fe and Oregon Trails, and as many as 6,000 to 12,000 are believed to have died on their way to the California gold fields in 1849. It is believed that over 150,000 Americans died during the pandemic between 1832 and 1849.

After their deaths, Lewis Starr and his wife were laid to rest in what became known to neighborhood residents as the *Davis-Smith Cemetery*. Their three sons married and migrated to Linn County, Oregon, between October 1853 and September 1854, securing 160-acres of free land for the settlement in that newly formed western territory.

Patentees (or, Original Land Owners) Section 15, Township 48, Range 32

Patentee	*Date*	*Certificate*	*Aliquots/Acres*
Davis, John	7/1/1845	23730	W½SW¼ / 80
Davis, John	7/1/1845	23733	W½NW¼
Brooking, Robert C.	7/1/1848	26816	SE¼NW¼
Davis, Joseph C.	7/1/1848	27014	NE¼SW¼ / 40
Cummings, Joseph	8/1/1849	28737	SE¼SE¼
Cummings, James W. (signee for **Matthew Davis, father of Elijah P. Davis**, late a Private in Captain Holder's Co., 12th Regiment, U.S. Infantry, [probably Mexican War]) 6/1/1850		20016	SE¼NE¼ & N½SE¼
Smith, Minor T.	2/15/1851	30701	NE¼NW¼
Davis, John (Private in Captain Berryman's Co., 11th Regiment, Kentucky Volunteers, War of 1812) **11/1/1851**		**6008**	**SE¼SW¼ / 40** (Cemetery)
Crabtree, James M.	10/2/1854	35543	NW¼NE¼
Crabtree, James M.	9/1/1856	45637	SW¼NE¼
Olds, Andrew J. J	6/1/1859	52688	NE¼NE¼

Sarah "Sally" Ann (Davis) Landers

John and Sarah "Sally" Davis were two of the earliest settlers in the Lost Township with John being listed as a farmer in the 1830 and 1840 U.S. Census having migrated from North Carolina. The Davis family eventually included nine children and seven slaves.[3] Davis was appointed one of the first county judges on the Jackson County Court on May 28, 1828. This was a legislative position, not a judicial seat. He would have been akin to a "county commissioner" or "county legislator."

In 1845, John Davis patented the first 40-acres of land in Section 15 in the Lost Township for $50.[4]

The1850 U.S. Census lists those living in the household of 81-year-old John Davis: his wife, Sarah "Sally," age 67, born in Tennessee; their children: Briscoe, 38, Jane, 21, Mary "Polly" (Davis) Cornett, 41, widow of John Cornett, and their children, Elizabeth Cornett, 21, Francis "Fannie" Cornett, 20; Darthula Cornett, 14, and, Jerusha Cornett, 12, and a Smith Crabtree, 16, is also listed as living in the household.

Sarah "Sally" Davis died in November 1850. John Davis died on or around October 13, 1853, according to his probate/estate file. And, while it is not recorded, *this couple is very likely buried in the Davis-Smith Cemetery.*

Their daughter, Sarah "Sally" Ann Davis, who had married James Landers on April 1, 1841, died June 14, 1851, and was buried

---

[3]The Davis children, according to genealogical research conducted by Roberta Bonnewitz from census and deeds included: 1) Joseph C. who married Anna; 2) Anderson, who married Hannah; 3) William (which may be the son Jefferson listed in John's Will); 4) Mary "Polly" who married John Cornett; 5) Briscoe who married Elizabeth Thomas; 6) Jesse who married Lucinda Thomas; 7) Susan Davis who married George Smith; 8) Sarah "Sally" who married James Landers; 9) Jerusha M. Davis who married Adam Hickman Smith. Seven slaves were reported on each of the two Censuses in 1830 and 1840.

[4] John Davis purchased on 1 July 1845, 80 acres in the W½SW¼; Certificate: 23730.

in the *Davis-Smith Cemetery*. She was just 30-years old; and had only been married for ten years when she passed away. James Landers subsequently married Winney Ann Cornett on November 16, 1851, who became the step-mother to Sally's children: John Briscoe Landers, age 9; Sarah J. Landers, 7; and, Alice A. Landers, 3.

After the death of John Davis, his son, Briscoe Davis, sold much of the Davis property in the Lost Township and moved to Westport, Missouri (today part of Kansas City, Missouri). By March 1857, siblings Briscoe, Jesse and Lucinda Davis had moved to Linn County, Kansas. However, by October of that same year the West Fork Baptist Church granted them letters of dismissal when they moved to Texas.

Some of the John Davis land in the Lost Township was sold to Martin Kritzer. Other portions of the Davis land went to the Smith family.

In the same year that Lewis Starr settled in Jackson County, another early settler, 22-year-old Adam Hickman Smith, claimed 80-acres of land nearby. Smith married the youngest child of John and Sarah "Sally" Davis, Jerusha M. Davis. The Smiths appear in the U.S. Census of Jackson County in 1850, 1860 and 1870.

On September 30, 1868, Jerusha M. Smith acquired additional acreage in the southeast ¼ of the southwest ¼ of Section 15, Township 48, Range 32 of Jackson County.[5]

By 1871, Adam Smith left in his Last Will and Testament 50-acres of land to his heirs in the Brooking Township. The area now known as Raytown, Missouri, located in Brooking Township was not even a town then, and Brooking Township was not formally established until 1872, having been formed from parts of Washington and Blue Townships. Smith stipulated in his Will that

---

[5] Jackson County Deeds, Book K, Page 40. This was in relation to the estate of Briscoe Davis estate, deceased September 30, 1868; Thomas C. Peers, administrator. Jerusha M. (Davis) Smith purchased 40 acres at $12/acre for a total of $480 at a private sale connected with this estate.

¼ of an acre be set aside as the *Davis Family Burying Grounds*, thus guaranteeing the perpetual preservation of this sacred spot.

This was confirmed when his wife, Jerusha M. Smith, sold the land to their children, Ann Elizabeth "Eliza" (Smith) Estes, Orin Briscoe Smith; and, Sallie Ann Smith, on December 14, 1871. She specifically set aside in the deed ¼-acre to include the *Davis Family Burying Grounds*, which was to be "reserved for a family burying ground forever."[6]

It was there that Lewis Starr and his wife had earlier been laid to rest. John and Sarah "Sally" Davis were also likely interred on this parcel before it was officially surveyed. And, as is fairly clear now, members of the Davis family married into the Smith family. Because of the strong connection between the two families, this plot of ground later became known as the *"Davis-Smith Cemetery,"* in recognition of these intermarrying, pioneer families.

Ann "Annie" (Starr) Crabtree

Another of the first settlers in the neighborhood were brothers Job and John Crabtree. Both came from Virginia in the year 1833. The first school of this area was built a mile south of the Crabtree home on the John Flanery farm. The first instructor was Isaac Crabtree. The school term was six months long, and for the purpose of computing tuition, each term was divided into two three-month sections. Tuition for each section was $2.50 per student. Sometimes part of the employment agreement was for the teacher to "board around" with various patrons and families. Boys normally attended school for only three or four months during the winter since their help was needed with farm chores the rest of the year. Girls and younger boys attended for two or three months in the spring.

---

[6] Jackson County Deeds, Book 93, Page 507.

Following his parents' deaths, Christopher Starr married a neighbor girl, Jane T. Crabtree, on February 27, 1848. Two years later his brother, John J. Starr, married Jane's sister, Matilda Crabtree, on April 6, 1851. The brother's sister, Annie Starr,", married Jane and Matilda's brother, James Monroe Crabtree, just a few short weeks later on April 27, 1851.[7] After years of farming next to her husband, Annie (Starr) Crabtree succumbed to either the hardships of pioneer life, or possibly childbirth, and was buried in the *Davis-Smith Cemetery*.

Matilda Starr, Christopher and John J. Starr's other sister, also married into the Crabtree family by marrying Jane and Matilda Crabtree's brother, Job Crabtree, Jr., October 19, 1851. Later, William H. Starr married Priscilla Crabtree on April 23, 1853.

Like many early settlers the Starr and Crabtree families became strongly connected through marriage and these strong filial relationships even engulfed their extended families and neighbors. A quote in the local newspaper described everyday life of the community. "Our neighbors were scattered, but we knew them all for miles around; the children by their given names; even the dogs and their horses were known to all of us."[8]

Gold had been discovered in California in January of 1848, and many an early settler caught the gold fever. News of the discovery brought some 300,000 people from the east, through Jackson County, to California. Soon after this Christopher, John, and William H. Starr joined the movement west; they went to the Oregon Territory for free land, as earlier noted. Their neighbor George Smith, who had married Susan Davis, left with fellow neighbor, Isaac Crabtree, and also headed to Oregon. Unfortunately, Isaac died on the way. Smith had started for Oregon a month early to arrange accommodations and to greet the others when they arrived.

---

[7] Jackson County marriage records also list James Monroe Crabtree marrying Elizabeth Davis on November 28, 1844.
[8] *Raytown News*, December 27, 1934.

According to the 1850 U.S. Census, George Smith, 42-years-old, from Tennessee, was listed as a "teamster." His wife, Susan (Davis) Smith, 33, was listed as having been born in Kentucky. All of their children were shown to be born in Missouri: Bersha, 19; Washington, 16; John S. 12; Armilda, 11; Elizabeth A., 9; and, Mary C., 2. Oregon donation land claims state that George Smith settled in Polk County, Oregon, having married "Susan" in Jackson County, Missouri, on July 11, 1830.

Jane (Billings) Davis

Other relatives of the John Davis family are buried in the *Davis-Smith Cemetery*. Forty-one-year-old Jane (Billings) Davis, may well have died in 1870 giving birth, an unfortunate but common occurrence among early pioneer women. A set of twins, Oby and Dee Davis, infant children, are recorded as being buried there with Jane. And, Jane's mother, remembered only as Mrs. Billings, is also buried beside her daughter.

Many similar deaths whose final dates remain unrecorded leave us to surmise that many young women died during childbirth or from the epidemics that often swept the country from various times. High infant mortality and minimal preparation for motherhood caused much anxiety in women as they tried to raise healthy children. Women wore themselves out through constant years of childbearing, because many couples began having children almost immediately after marriage, and continued rearing children at fairly close intervals for 15 or 20 years. Couples had as many children as possible, knowing that not all would survive their first years. After having born several children, pioneer women usually became ill from childbirth or run down from managing the family. The life expectancy for women then at 43 was only higher by two years than a man's, but the risks associated with childbirth in those times before modern obstetrics caused a woman's mortality rate to be fifteen times higher.

Early Raytown and its Faithful Citizens

At its inception Raytown was but a village with about half a dozen houses, a general store and post office, where citizens got their mail once a week. There was William Ray's blacksmith shop, Dr. Minor T. Smith's home, a small one-room school house and one other small residence. Most of the citizens were farmers. It was prosperous farming country having good land, water, and timber, three necessities not always found all together. Many claimed there were more good springs in this township than in any other comparable community in the state. An early settler boasted that the farmers there had not had to drive their stock off their farms to get water for them in the last twenty-five years.

William Ray, one of the earliest settlers in the community owned the blacksmith shop in the town that later held his name. Ray was given credit for founding the city before he joined his neighbors for the California gold fields shortly after his wife's death in 1849. The community offered a last chance to westward-bound settlers for refitting and resupply before setting out for the Santa Fe, Oregon and California Trails. Ray repaired wagons, and had a reputation for making ox shoes and fitting them securely.

The land surrounding

Valley of the Little Blue River

Raytown bountifully produced beans, potatoes, wheat, corn, oats and hay. A good number of the farms also made butter to sell and every farm had an orchard attached. The majority of the small farms had at least 20 to 30 acres in cultivation. George Washington Wells a farmer whose home was in the valley of the Little Blue was credited with "growing cotton, wheat and anything that grew well." Most farmers raised sheep, oxen and cattle besides horses. Hogs were raised and after slaughtering and salting were sent to the military forts further west. Records show that good sized shipments of honey and bees wax was shipped to St. Louis.

The customs of trading farm produce for store items, or for the doctor's, teacher's or preacher's services lasted for several generations. More costly luxury items came by ship to New Orleans then up the river to St. Louis then by steamboat to Kansas City then overland to the stores. It was only occasionally that the farmers would venture into town. What they needed or produced was to be had on their own farms or those of their neighbors.

One of the first orders of business as other settlers began arriving was establishing a place of worship. The fabric of Missouri society was comprised of hard-working, God-fearing men and women who came to the state as pioneers and developed the land into prosperous farms. They built fine homes and started businesses. Their Bibles represented their moral code, a standard with which to judge themselves and their neighbors. As soon as they raised a roof over their heads their thoughts quickly turned to building a place for worship. They looked forward to expressing their freedom of religion established by the Founding Fathers and guaranteed in the Constitution that they loved so dear. Churches provided bedrock foundations for their communities. They were the safe harbors during troubled times. They assured their members that, despite the uncertainty and upheaval around them, there was still a God who comforted and cared for them.

Several families began meeting in the home of John Davis before deciding to build a permanent building. The first church was established in Davis's home on December 10, 1842. No one would have dreamed at the time of the impact of that first decision made in the community. When the church was first established, it had 17 members: 7 families and 2 individuals.

It was in 1799 that Daniel Boone, the famous pioneer, had followed his son, Daniel Morgan Boone, to Missouri. In March 1844, Boone's grandsons, Daniel and Morgan Boone, then residing in Jackson County, were asked to build the first church building in the Lost Township. It was named the West Fork of the Little Blue Baptist Church and was made from native stone on two acres of land. It was a rectangular structure, 20-feet-wide by 24-feet-long with a low ceiling. The construction expense was borne by local businessmen, Alvin Brooking, J. Mickleborough, and Archibald Rice.

Sometimes the ride to church would take an hour or two depending on how far away one lived. Roads were few and poorly maintained in those days.

In 1859, a second church building was built of brick on the same ground, replacing the original stone structure. The two main doors of the building were built not to segregate the races but to segregate the sexes. Of the handful of church members at the start of the war, 25 were slaves. Slaves were eligible for membership and attended services alongside their masters.

The original members of the first church were all prominent citizens of the area. By 1880, there were more than 170 members. From the first sixteen charter members of the West Fork of the Little Blue Baptist Church in Raytown, Missouri, the church has now grown to thousands, being one of the largest of its denomination in the State.

1859 West Fork of the Little Blue Baptist Church

Other prominent church members were men like Richard Marshall Fristoe, a church deacon, who was the first Presiding Judge on the Jackson County Court. He was also the maternal grandfather of Thomas Coleman "Cole" Younger, and was a grandnephew of Chief Justice John Marshall of Virginia. He had fought alongside Andrew Jackson at the battle of New Orleans during the War of 1812, and it was through his efforts that Jackson County was named after his commanding officer. Cole Younger's great-grandmother on his father's side was a daughter of Lighthorse Harry Lee of Revolutionary War fame. Richard Marshall Fristoe and his son-in-law, Henry Washington Younger, owned several large tracts of land in the area. He was well known in the area for having fish and wild game traps which kept his table well supplied. His wife was reared in luxury, yet on the western frontier she was content to live in their

28

log cabin home. Besides Fristoe, two other of Jackson County's first County Court Judges were charter members of the West Fork church: Alvin Brooking, and previously mentioned John Davis. Alvin Brooking, a founding member of the West Fork Baptist Church, was also a State senator representing Jackson and Van Buren Counties (later re-named Cass County) as well as being a trustee of the newly formed William Jewell College in Liberty.

The treatment of slaves among the settlers in the Lost Township was little known to those who lived outside the area. Of the small percentage of landowners who owned slaves, small farms sometimes had at least a couple of slaves while the largest farms consisting of several hundred acres operated with between 20-25 slaves. Slave families were always kept together and the evidence of early Wills shows that in many instances property was divided amongst the heirs as well as their slaves. Some Wills of the time stipulated that money left in estates go for the expenses of keeping their former slaves.

Descendants of Reuben Marshall Harris, Sr.

Local citizen Reuben Marshall Harris, Sr., was born about 1760 in Buckingham County, Virginia. He married Margaret "Peggy" (Alexander) Harris and they had 11 children in Patrick County, Virginia, before settling in Jackson County, Missouri, by 1830. After Peggy died, Reuben married Elizabeth Gray in Jackson County, and they had five children. Reuben probably died on March 18, 1842, according to his probate/estate file;[9] and his widow re-married to Samuel Mann in 1847.

Buried in the *Davis-Smith Cemetery* are several descendants of Reuben Marshall and Margaret "Peggy" (Alexander) Harris, Sr., though a reason why this family would have been concentrated in this small burying ground remains a mystery.

---

[9] Meador, Victor P. *Jackson County Wills and Administrations, 1828-1862.* (Independence, Mo.: Jackson County Genealogical Society), 22-23.

Mahala (Harris) and William Allen Slusher
(daughter and son-in-law of Reuben Marshall Harris, Sr.)

William Allen Slusher and his wife Mahala (Harris) Slusher, are both buried in the *Davis-Smith Cemetery*. Around 1840, Slusher built a water mill and a saw mill over the Little Blue River. William died in October, 1842. His wife, Mahala, was 33 when she died on February 1, 1843. After Mahala's death she left behind four young children. Out of necessity, the young children were split up and taken in by different friends and relations.[10] The County Court ordered the guardians of the children to dispose of their mother's property, but were allowed to keep their mother's wearing apparel, a trunk and a bolt of cloth made for clothing the children.

Margaret "Peggy" (Harris) Taylor
(daughter of Reuben Marshall Harris, Sr.)

Margaret "Peggy" Harris was born between 1810 and 1812 in Patrick County, Virginia. She married Creed Taylor on July 15, 1832, in Jackson County, Missouri. It was recalled in 1933 that Peggy died in 1869 at age 61. Peggy is buried in the *Davis-Smith Cemetery*.

Laura Matilda (Fristoe) Harris
(daughter-in-law of Reuben Marshall Harris, Sr.)

Reuben Marshall Harris, Jr., another West Fork Baptist Church member, married Laura Matilda Fristoe on June 13, 1833. Laura was born February 20, 1818, and brought to Missouri

---

[10] Wilburne Slusher was appointed to Samuel Harris as guardian; Julia Ann Slusher to William Hockensmith; Virginia Slusher to Creed Taylor; and, Mahala Slusher to Austin and Lucy (Harris) Boothe, her aunt and uncle. From Meador's *Jackson County Wills*.

Territory when she was two months old by her parents, Judge Richard Marshall and Polly L. Fristoe.[11]

Reuben Marshall Harris, Jr., had a horse-drawn gristmill where area farmers came to get their corn and wheat ground into flour. It was a great convenience to the surrounding farmers even though it did not make a great deal of profit. Reuben Marshall and Laura Matilda Harris, Jr., were also the parents of Civil War guerrilla Thomas B. Harris; as well as in-laws to guerrilla, Nathan B. Kerr. They were also the aunt and uncle to brothers John and Jabez McCorkle, and Cole Younger, all known Civil War guerrillas. They all lived along the hills above the Little Blue River just a few miles south of Independence. When Laura Matilda (Fristoe) Harris died, she was buried in the *Davis-Smith Cemetery*, with several other Harris family relatives.

Mary Ellen (Harris) Tucker
(granddaughter of Reuben Marshall Harris, Sr.)

Laura Matilda Harris's daughter, Mary Ellen (Harris) Tucker, was born March 23, 1834, and married to Elisha Tucker on May 8, 1853. The couple lived in Lone Jack when the 1860 U.S. Census was taken, and Elisha was listed as an engineer. Mary Ellen died on October 13, 1869, and was buried in the *Davis-Smith Cemetery* with other Harris relatives. At her death at thirty-five years old she left a husband and two teenage daughters, who appeared in the 1870 U.S. Census in Lee's Summit, where Mr. Tucker was listed as a 43-year-old farmer from Virginia.

---

[11] Meador, 40. They had six children: 1) Bersheba Fristoe, who married Henry "Harry" Washington Younger (they became the parents of 12 children, including Coleman "Cole" Younger); 2) Lavina (Laura); 3) Mary Ann; 4) Thomas J.; 5) Nancy B.; and, 6) Francis C.

Bersheba Ann (Harris) & Richard Sly, Sr.
(granddaughter of Reuben Marshall Harris, Sr.)

Richard Sly, Sr., was born on March 23, 1834, and died on October 28, 1853. He was remembered in 1933 as having been buried in the *Davis-Smith Cemetery*.[12] Richard Sly and Bersheba Ann Harris were married on May 8, 1853. Sly was only married for five months before passing away unexpectedly. Their youngest son, Richard Sly, Jr. went to live with his brother-in-law, Reuben Marshall Harris, Jr., as recorded in the 1860 U.S. Census.

Civil War Looms

Despite the hardships, the early local pioneers continued in their pursuits, buying and selling, living and dying, endeavoring to make a better life for their children than what they had known. Many of these Jackson County settlers had become quite prosperous. As the decade of the 1850's began to wane, the slavery issue became more and more volatile throughout the country, but especially in Jackson County. For the past several years, Kansas abolitionists and freesoilers had been entering the county spying out the farms and property of wealthy landowners. When war came the world of these prosperous citizens was suddenly turned upside down. The hard times and scarcity of money restricted the purchase of grain and hay. Failure of crops thwarted the purchase of lumber for buildings.

The uncertainty of the times compelled many settlers to seek safer environs. Jesse Davis, son of early settler, John Davis, took his family to Linn County, Kansas, in 1857. Linn County was home to the original Kansas Jayhawkers nearer to the start of the Civil War.

---

[12]According to the DAR's 1934 compendium, it may be that Richard Sly is actually buried in the Campground Cemetery, another pioneer cemetery were other members of the Harris family are interred.

Their depredations eventually drove Davis back into Jackson County, Missouri, before he decided to take his family to Texas in August 1861. He didn't return until the War was over.

At the start of the Civil War, most young men in the area had gone south to enlist under General Sterling Price in the Missouri State Guards. Missouri had initially wished to remain neutral.

When Union General Nathaniel Lyon issued a declaration of war on the sovereign state of Missouri, Governor Claiborne Jackson issued a call for volunteers to protect Missouri and to keep outside troops from entering the state.

Because of the strength of the Missouri State Guard and the concern of Missouri seceding from the Union, federal troops from Kansas, Iowa, Indiana and Illinois were dispatched to Missouri. The first several battles at Carthage, Wilson's Creek and Lexington resulting in Southern victories cemented the fact that it would be a long protracted war. Though Missouri was initially successful in keeping the state neutral massive numbers of Federal troops, German and Irish mercenaries soon arrived forcing Price's army further into southern Missouri. Realizing that they could not face these overpowering odds alone the Missouri Legislature that had been run out of the capitol by Federal forces met in Neosho, Missouri, and on October 31, 1861, voted to join the Confederacy.

In Jackson County, nerves were on edge. With many young men gone south with General Sterling Price, Kansas Jayhawkers swept across the border burning, looting and murdering anyone with Southern sympathies.

One man rose to the forefront as a leader to protect the lives and property of those left behind. On January 1, 1862, William Clarke Quantrill gathered around him a small band of men to confront the atrocities of the Kansas Jayhawkers. Those from Jackson County suffered the most and many young men from the Lost Township and neighboring townships eagerly rushed to join Quantrill to fight as guerrillas against the Federal occupation. The men and boys from the Lost Township represented the best of

Quantrill's company and each had their own story to tell of some brutal Jayhawker raid.

On October 27, 1861, Jayhawkers burned the home of Martin Flanery, who then joined Quantrill. Flanery reported that Charles Jennison's Jayhawkers had burned a church and twenty-seven other homes in the neighborhood and had pillaged the home of Reuben Marshall Harris, Jr., in the middle of the night. These Jayhawker raids left the pro-Southern farmers stunned.

Harris had been a school teacher and a revenue officer before the war. He owned a gristmill at the Little Blue River. Jayhawkers set fire to his home and mill in the summer of 1863 and burned it so that the area farmers had to go to Kansas City to buy their flour.

Harris's wife, Laura, and their other small children were home at the time. Their daughter, Nancy "Nannie" Elizabeth Ellen, had married Jabez McCorkle, one of Quantrill's men, and was also living in the Harris home.[13]

The attack by the Jayhawkers on the Harris home was devastating:

> "*The door to Mrs. McCorkle's room on the first floor was broken open and a squad of noisy Jayhawkers rushed into the apartment. The alarmed lady entreated them to retire until she could put on her clothes, but they cursed her and told her to get up and pretty damn quick or they would prod her with their sabers. A bright fire was burning in the open hearth; the wretches took blazing brands and carried them as they ransacked the closets, dresser drawers and trunks. A little girl (either three-year-old Virginia or six-year-old Eliza) was sleeping with her mother, was awakened by the unusual noise and began to cry, and one of the men went to her and,*

---

[13] Cole Younger, nephew of Reuben and Laura Harris, was an officer in Quantrill's company. Petersen, Paul. *Quantrill of Missouri: The Making of a Guerrilla Warrior: The Man, The Myth, The Soldier.* (Nashville, TN: Cumberland House, 2003), 67.

holding a saber against her face, told her if she uttered another sound he would cut her head off. The poor thing was so frightened and subdued that she did not utter a word for days. The young girls who were sleeping upstairs were aroused by the disturbance below hastily dressed and ran to their mother's room. The outlaws then turned their attention to the girls, using insulting terms, searched their persons for valuables, and all the while singing ribald songs or telling obscene jokes. They took from the pocket in the housemaid's petticoat forty dollars, tearing the apparel from the person. The creatures made the girls go before them as they searched every apartment in the house, from which they purloined every article of value they could carry. Then returning downstairs three of the wretches took by force three of the girls into the yard and marched them back and forth in the moonlight, making most vicious threats and insinuations. After several hours of this atrocious conduct the creatures started away."[14]

Another report of this cruel incident stated that:

"In Brooking Township, six miles south of Independence, along the valley of the Little Blue, Jayhawkers paid a visit to the home of Reuben M. Harris, an uncle of Coleman Younger. They had raided the property before [October 1861], but this time they wanted to complete the destruction. Only a month earlier they had tried to murder one of Reuben's daughters, eighteen-year-old Nannie Harris, in the collapse of the Kansas City prison. Now they stole everything of value and burned the house. One daughter asleep upstairs was rescued from the flames by her sister. As the raiders left,

---

[14] Petersen, 67 and 324. A granddaughter of Reuben and Laura, Frances (Deal) Helm, wrote in 1964 that, "two slaves owned by my grandparents had run into the woods and hid.... With a quilt that had been overlooked and [a pair of old oxen] pulling the surrey, they set out for Howard County, Missouri, 100 miles away. My Grandfather was crippled and walked with one crutch. [They] with five small grandchildren...rode, and the rest walked.

one of them shouted at Mrs. Harris, "Now, old lady, call on your protectors. Why don't you call on Cole Younger now?"

During these tumultuous times the Lost Township had an anchor in the storm. The cornerstone of the Lost Township community was the West Fork of the Little Blue Baptist Church. Southern churches had many problems to contend with during the war. Most tried to remain neutral, but when Lincoln called for a day of fasting and prayer on behalf of the Union cause, the request was considered coercion by many in Missouri. The animosity aroused by the Presidential proclamation caused many congregations to split or disband. Like many church pastors in the area, Jeremiah Farmer was Southern in his sympathies. He conducted church services not only in the West Fork of the Little Blue Baptist Church but rode a wide circuit in Missouri from Westport to Oak Grove, leading evangelistic services.

When Lincoln asked church leaders to recite designed prayers for divine supplication to the continued unity of the Federal government and to the health of the President of the United States, the West Fork Baptist Church decided to close its doors for the duration of the hostilities. From August 1862, following the First Battle of Independence to June 1866, there are no church records for the West Fork of the Little Blue Baptist Church.)[15]

Virginia C. "Kate" Harris
(granddaughter of Reuben Marshall Harris, Sr.)

Virginia C. "Kate" Harris, born December 22, 1856, met an untimely death when at only 23 years old she was struck by lightning. She was one of the last burials for many years to come, being laid to rest in the *Davis-Smith Cemetery* on March 11, 1879.[16]

---

[15] Brooks, Paul. *Legacy of Faith*, 36-37.

[16] The Virginia mentioned in the section above relates to the child of Reuben Marshall and Laura (Fristoe) Harris, who was born December 22, 1856. Given that another note by Harris descendants pointed to an 1880 death, at this writing, it is

Captain Ferdinand Marion Scott
and Daniel Boone Scholl

Despite the trying times of Civil War friends and neighbors banded together to protect what was left of their way of life. Neighbor Benjamin Rice, associated with the West Fork Baptist Church and a guerrilla fighter with Quantrill, was called upon to help patrol the roads leading from Kansas to alert the citizens if he spied any signs of Jayhawkers approaching. Benjamin Rice lost his slaves and much of his property during the war to ruthless marauders.[17] Rice's neighbor, 24-year-old Boone T. Muir, rode with him in Quantrill's ranks. Muir was the great grandson of Daniel Boone, the famed pioneer.

Another neighbor was John T. House. House was 23- years-old when Jayhawkers rampaged through his neighborhood. His father, Ephraim Eli House, lived on a farm close by. Both men were God-fearing pioneers, being charter members of the West Fork of the Little Blue Baptist Church. When Jayhawker Colonel Charles Jennison saw the elder House working in a wooded area, he asked where his sympathies lay. The farmer told him he favored the South, so Jennison murdered him then burned his house and drove away his livestock. At the time his son John was on duty with the Missouri State Guards. When he discovered that his father had been murdered by Jayhawkers, he returned home and joined Quantrill.

---

believed that the recollection of two separate burials recorded in the DAR's *Vital Historical Records*, that of Virginia Harris and of Kate Harris, may have been the same person. Reuben and Laura's granddaughter, Frances (Deal) Helm, wrote in 1964 about the Harris family exodus from Jackson County to Howard County, Missouri, and mentioned her aunt, Virginia "Kate" Harris (later killed by lightning).
[17] When Federals burned Rice's home, his wife, Jane, realizing she had left her baby in the house, rushed back in and rescued the child who escaped with singed hair. Benjamin Rice's uncle and aunt, Archibald and Sally Rice (who died in Jackson County in 1849 and 1853 respectively), were early settlers who owned a sizable plantation, including several log slave cabins. Archibald and Sally Rice's home and one slave cabin survives today (2011), as the Rice-Tremonti Home in Raytown.

John T. House and family, ca. 1881

With so many Jayhawker raids and Union patrols in Jackson County Quantrill established camps throughout the area surrounding the Lost Township during 1862. The area was inundated with open fields surrounded by rocky bluffs. The valley of the Little Blue River was a long narrow valley surrounded by heavy timber with a long ridge of rock outcroppings. The fertile valley and rolling hills marked an area that was superbly suited for hideaways and ambushes. Dense vegetation lay all along the riverbanks. To the southwest was White Oak Creek, one of the Little Blue's tributaries.

Situated in the narrow valley was the picturesque hamlet of Little Blue. The area had little besides a store, a post office, and a blacksmith shop. The Little Blue River supplied water to the area farmers and divided the higher area of the Lost Township to the west from the bottomland surrounding the river from the opposite bank toward Lee's Summit.

Year by year the Federal forces grew frustrated at not being able to capture or kill the elusive Quantrill and his band. Union troops suffered many an embarrassing defeat at the hands of the cunning guerrillas. In their ardor to crush out partisan warfare, Jawhawker cruelty and brutality increased. As the Jayhawkers resorted to terrorism, the guerrillas practiced the old dispensation over the new: Instead of turning the other cheek, it was now an eye for an eye and a tooth for a tooth.

The Federal's most embarrassing encounter came on June 17, 1863. Two companies of Kansas Jayhawkers were traveling from Paola, Kansas, to Union General Thomas Ewing's headquarters in Kansas City, Missouri. As they were making their way along the Westport to Kansas City road they were ambushed by seventy of Quantrill's men under the leadership of Captain George Todd.

Four miles south of Kansas City, near Westport, on the road leading to Kansas City, Todd saw a column of blue uniforms. On the southeast side of Westport was a lane bordered by a tall rock fence on either side. As the guerrillas entered the lane, Todd deployed his men into platoons of eight on both sides of the road. Each man knew what was to be done. The column approaching them was led by Captain Henry Flesher. Flesher reported that he was surprised by a large force of guerrillas that was concealed behind stone fences, which were half-hidden in thick underbrush and dense foliage that lined either side of the road. Quantrill's scout John McCorkle noted: *"They came riding very leisurely over the hill, the captain in front, with his leg thrown over his horse's neck." As soon as Flesher discovered blue-uniformed soldiers on his flanks, he called out and demanded to know who they were. In reply Todd gave the signal to set off the ambush, shouting, "Charge, kill 'em, boys, kill 'em!"*

With pistols blazing, the guerrillas attacked. Charging horses kicked up so much dust on the road that it was hard to tell friend from foe. The attack was so sudden, and the first volley so rapidly followed by a charge of mounted guerrillas, that the Federals were forced back until they reached an open space where they could reform. Todd had with him many of Quantrill's best men. Besides Ferdinand Scott were John Jarrette, Dick Yeager, Bill Anderson, William Gregg, Richard Berry, Dick and George T. Maddox, Alson

Wyatt, Will McGuire, John McCorkle, Boone T. Muir, George and Boone Scholl, Frank and Jesse James, and Fletcher Taylor. Scholl had killed four of the enemy before he was shot out of the saddle. His horse was new, and in the rush of the charge, he lost control of it, and the animal ran with him through the Federal lines. A Union soldier shot him in the back, and the bullet passed through his body, breaking the buckle of his belt.

Daniel Boone Scholl was taken back to the Lost Township and buried in the *Davis-Smith Cemetery*. Scholl was a cousin of guerrilla, Boone T. Muir, and rode beside him before Scholl's death. Scholl, a great grandson of pioneer Daniel Boone, left behind a brother, George Thomas Scholl, who continued riding with the guerrillas.[18]

Fletcher Taylor claimed that he killed five Federal troops with as many shots. Bill Anderson was seen in the thick of the battle and was described as a tiger unloosed. Jarrette found himself surrounded by three Federals, all shooting at him simultaneously. Untouched by their

Daniel Boone Scholl was shot to death and buried in the *Davis-Smith Cemetery*

rounds, he killed all three. Flesher reported thirty-three men killed or wounded. The rest of his command put spurs to their horses and tried to make it to the safety of Kansas City. A short distance beyond, a regiment of Federal infantry emerged from the shelter of the woods to succor their retreating comrades.

---

[18] Scholl was born on May 30, 1843, in Clark Co. Ky. He was killed while leading the charge at the Westport skirmish on June 17, 1863.

Ferdinand Scott led the pursuit of the fleeing Federals, and because he was gaily dressed, was singled out by their sharpshooters. As the guerrillas drew rein observing the Federals at a safe distance, a Union sniper, shot Scott through the neck. He threw up his hands and exclaimed, "I am a dead man," and fell from his horse. This was a great loss to Quantrill's company. Scott was much loved by his men. He talked little, showed little emotion, and never showed any physical fear. Others have added that he was tenderhearted, true to his ideals of patriotism above everything else, and that nothing deterred him in the line of duty.

Scott was born in 1840. He was originally from Ohio before moving to Liberty in Clay County, Missouri, in 1858, where he was employed as a saddle maker. He married Josephine Vance on May 20, 1861. Scott's name was listed on Quantrill's July 6, 1862, company muster roll assigned as the commissary sergeant. Scott took part in several early skirmishes eventually becoming a captain. On August 11, 1862, he took a conspicuous part in the first Battle of Independence and also at the battle of Lone Jack on August 15. On May 19, 1863, Scott led twelve guerrillas on a raid near Missouri City and ambushed an entire company of Federals. He was described by author John Newman Edwards in *Noted Guerrillas*: *"Perhaps by nature and temperament, no man was better fitted for the life of a guerrilla than Ferdinand Scott. Under fire no soldier could be cooler. He won the love of his men first and later their devotion."* They buried Scott in his saddle blanket next to his friend Daniel Boone Scholl.

Scholl was born on May 30, 1843, in Kentucky and was only 21–years-old when he was killed. His parents were Nelson and Harriet Wright (Boone) Scholl. She was the daughter of Rev. Thomas and Sarah "Sallie" (Muir) Boone. Scholl's grandparents were Septimus and Sarah "Sallie" (Miller) Scholl, who had lived thirty years in Clark County, Kentucky, before immigrating to Jackson County in September 1844. Daniel Boone Scholl was also a great grandson of Daniel Boone. Scholl joined Co A, of the 1st Missouri Cavalry and rode with them from June 10, 1861, to January 2, 1862, then like many other young men of the neighborhood came home and served under Quantrill.

The guerrillas lost one other man, Alson Wyatt who was mortally wounded and taken to a relative's home where he died the next day.[19] Wyatt was only 22-years-old when he was killed.

Of all the names recorded in 1933 of those having been buried in the *Davis-Smith Cemetery*, only one has been called into question. Boone T. Muir is incorrectly reported as having been killed on June, 17, 1863, in the Westport skirmish. In fact, it was his cousin, Daniel Boone Scholl, who was killed on that date, and buried in the *Davis-Smith Cemetery*. Boone T. Muir survived the War and moved to Texas, but returned to Missouri shortly before his death. Muir died at the Masonic Home in St. Louis on May 7, 1916, and is buried in the Belton City Cemetery in Cass County, Missouri.

Charity (McCorkle) Kerr; sisters Susan (Crawford) Vandevere, and Armenia (Crawford) Selvey
(granddaughters of Reuben Marshall Harris, Sr.)

Seeking retaliation for the recent defeat at the hands of Quantrill's guerrillas General Thomas Ewing issued orders for the arrest of the guerrillas' female relatives.

Nancy "Nannie" Elizabeth Ellen Harris related that after the Redlegs (or Kansas Jayhawkers) set fire to her home and wrecked her family's gristmill over the Little Blue River in the early summer of 1863, she had to buy flour and supplies in Kansas City. There were Bushwhackers in the Sni Hills and all through Jackson County, and the Union men believed that the women were smuggling arms and ammunition to them...but that wasn't so, according to Harris. They did, however, smuggle food under their hoop skirts and buggy

---

[19] Petersen, 151, 245.

seats. She said the menfolk were always able to get ammunition without help from the women.

Harris recalled going to Kansas City with her sister-in-law, Charity (McCorkle) Kerr, in July 1863. They drove a wagon led by a yoke of oxen fifteen miles to Kansas City in order to exchange their wheat for flour and other purchases, which they put into a satchel.

Along their journey, they were arrested and incarcerated with other young, Southern women. A neighbor, Anderson Cowgill, had told officers that the girls were rebels and were feeding bushwhackers. The youngest of these was only 10-years-old. Others were mothers of families forced to leave their young children behind.

They were held at guard to await sentencing and banishment from the area in a three-story, brick building commandeered by the Federals from its owner, George Caleb Bingham, who was serving as Provisional State Treasurer in Jefferson City, Missouri. This makeshift Union jail was located at 1425 Grand Avenue, in downtown Kansas City (today, the Sprint Arena occupies this historic block).

After only a few days imprisonment, soldiers from the 11th Kansas Jayhawker Regiment, commanded by General Ewing and serving as their prison guards, undermined the building's foundation causing it to collapse on August 13, 1863.[20]

Mrs. Mattie Lykins, wife of noted Kansas City doctor, Johnston Lykins, was at the scene that day. After the death of her husband, Mattie married "Missouri's Painter," General George Caleb Bingham, and wrote the following recollection before her death in 1890:

> *. . . during the war many southern women were arrested and imprisoned on suspicion of aiding and abetting the Confederate cause. As a place of imprisonment for such in*

[20] Hale, Donald R. *Branded as Rebels*, 250; also, *Kansas City* (Mo.) *Journal*, 14 and 15 Aug. 1863; and, *Kansas City* (Mo.) *Post*, 2 May 1912.

this city, an old dilapidated brick building on the levee once known and used as the Mechanics Bank, was taken possession of by the military authorities and set apart as a prison for Rebel women. After the building had been occupied as such for some time it became so infested with rats and vermin of all kinds as to render it unfit for human beings to live in. Even the health of the guards, who had access to the river for bathing, suffered so much from the stench and torture of the vermin as to lead them to appeal to headquarters for a change of location.

According to their request, a building was selected which stood about the middle of a block of brick buildings known as the Metropolitan Block on Grand Avenue between 13th and 14th Streets. The house selected belonged to General Bingham [George Caleb Bingham] who at that time was treasurer of the state and living in Jefferson City, Missouri]. For more than six years previous to the war, General Bingham had lived in Europe. The death of several near relatives led him to return to this country with some large paintings unfinished which he had been commissioned by the legislature of this state to paint for the capitol building at Jeff City. For the purpose of finishing these large paintings it was necessary for him to have a studio with light unobstructed by surrounding objects. Hence, some months before he left Europe, he wrote to a party in this city to have a competent architect examine his building in the Metropolitan Block on Grand Avenue and if thought to be strong enough to bear the weight of an additional story twenty feet high to have the story added to the building. The opinion of the architect being favorable, it was ready for General Bingham on his return. He continued to occupy the building both as a studio and residence until appointed by President Lincoln, treasurer of the state, which office had suddenly been made vacant by the flight of Gov. [Claiborne] Jackson and his cabinet to the Confederate States.

General Thomas Ewing was then in command of this military district with headquarters at Kansas City. He did not notify General Bingham that his building was needed for a prison, but simply took possession of it and ordered the women prisoners transferred to it and confined in the third story which General Bingham had used for his studio.

The Metropolitan Block was so constructed that the sleepers [horizontal beams] of the floors served the purpose of braces to the dividing walls of each building. The sleepers of the first floor rested on brick pillars in the cellar. In the exciting events of the times our citizens had forgotten the imprisoned women until one hot day, Friday, August 14th, about two o'clock, this prison fell, burying beneath its walls a number of its inmates, four of whom were dreadfully mangled and crushed to death. Others had limbs broken or dislocated. I was told that on investigation it was learned, (and I think this testimony may be found on file in the Claim Department of the War office in Washington City), that the building had been weakened by the removal of the brick pillars which supported the first floor, and further that some of the sleepers of the adjoining buildings on both sides had also been removed, thus weakening the dividing walls beyond safety. By whom this inhuman act was done, was not known, for what purpose, was left to conjecture.

In less than an hour after this building fell, I was informed by some of the women prisoners that they had repeatedly been told by their guards that the house was giving away and would eventually fall. "But," they said, "We had so often been told during our imprisonment, equally as alarming stories which proved false, that we paid no attention to this one, yet, every few days we heard the building crack, which was invariably followed by the falling of pieces of plastering from the ceiling."

Dr. Joshua Thorne, who still lives in our City, was at that time chief surgeon of the hospital at this place. While I stood

45

beside him, near the building, watching the removal of the living and the dead from the debris, some one remarked to him that they supposed some of the soldiers on guard would be found buried beneath the ruins. "No," replied Dr. Thorne, "Not a blue coat will be found; every man who has been detailed to stand guard at this prison for the last few weeks, knew the house to be unsafe and have kept themselves at a safe distance from the trembling walls. I knew the building to be unsafe," he continued, "and notified the military authorities of the fact, and suggested the removal of the women prisoners, but my suggestion was not heeded. Before you is the result."[21]

The afternoon of the collapse some of the girls were seated around the bed of Charity (McCorkle) Kerr, who had developed a fever due to exposure and improper diet. Her cousin asked the guard for some water. Charity was being closely cared from by Mary Ann "Molly" Granstaff, who was fixing her hair.[22] Several of the girls sat on the floor and watched. Ten-year-old Martha Anderson had angered the guards the day before, and in retaliation they chained a 12-pound ball to her ankle. The girls sitting around Charity's bed saw the ceiling begin to crack, sending debris down upon the women. Sensing imminent danger, they tried desperately to get out of the building. Nancy "Nannie" Elizabeth Ellen Harris and Molly Anderson went into the hallway to wait for the guard to return with water.

---

[21] Bingham, Martha A. "Mattie" (Livingston) Lykins. "Recollections of Old Times in Kansas City," 67-page handwritten manuscript, ca 1883 - 1890. Gift of Robert Dewit Owen, in memory of his grandmother, Mrs. Dewit Livingston (Ada Armintha Campbell) Owen, Jackson County Historical Society Archives, Independence, Missouri, Document ID 110F7.

[22] Granstaff (or Grandstaff), then age 23, with several broken bones and injured back, was the last to be rescued. She was shuffled to St. Louis as Union troops suspected a rescue. Her ambulance was upset along the way causing her additional injuries. She later married William J. Clay. She died in 1915, and is buried in Mount Washington Cemetery. *Kansas City* (Mo.) *Post*, 5 Mar 1915. Missouri Death Certificate.

Nancy "Nannie" Elizabeth Ellen (Harris) McCorkle (later Lilley)

Charity (McCorkle) Kerr

They heard the other girls shout that the roof was falling. The structure began to fall as the guard was returning.

Five of the dozen women died; four were crushed to death instantly: Charity (McCorkle) Kerr; Susan (Crawford) Vandevere; Armenia (Crawford) Selvey, and, Josephine Anderson. Another victim, Mrs. Wilson, died a few days later from wounds received in the collapse. Others escaped with only mangled bodies each carrying emotional and physical scars for the rest of their lives.

The youngest victim was Josephine Anderson, the 14-year-old sister of Captain Bill Anderson. For a long time her cries were heard calling for anyone to take the bricks off of her head. Finally her cries went silent. Her body was taken a few miles back to where she had been staying with friends and buried in the Union Cemetery in Kansas City. Two other of Anderson's sisters survived, but were maimed in the collapse.

Guerrilla, Riley Crawford, a nephew of Reuben Marshall Harris, lost two sisters in the jail massacre. Thirty-one year old Susan (Crawford) Vandevere, whose husband Thomas rode with Quantrill, was killed in the collapse. Susan was first married to William N. Whitsett on March 25, 1853. After his death, she married Thomas Vandevere on March 9, 1856.[23] Thomas was

---

[23] The couple were listed in the household of Rhoda Harris, the widow of William Harris, who was a brother of Reuben Marshall Harris, Sr., when the 1860 U.S. Census for Blue Springs, Jackson County, Missouri, was conducted. Thomas was a 41-year-old Indiana native. Susan (Crawford) Vandever was 26.

reported "missing-in-action" during the War and all trace of him was lost. Susan's murder at age 29 left four small children orphaned without a mother or father.[24]

Susan's sister, Armenia (Crawford) Selvey, was also killed in the Union jail collapse. She was just 27–years-old at the time of the unfortunate incident.[25] Armenia married Charles Selvey on February 28, 1854. The couple appeared in the 1860 U.S. Census for Blue Springs, Jackson County, Missouri, with their children, who were all under the age of nine when she was killed.[26]. Susan and Armenia were the daughters of Elizabeth "Betsy" (Harris) and Jeptha M. Crawford;[27] Betsy being a daughter of Reuben Marshall and Laura (Fristoe) Harris, Jr.

---

[24] They were, Armina, 5; Jeptha, 3; Thomas, 1; and, Laura, 11 months old (ages from the 1860 U.S. Census.

[25] Arminia was 24 when the 1860 U.S. Census was enumerated.

[26] In 1860 the children were Jeptha, age 6; Lewis, 4; and Rowland, 2.

[27] Jeptha M. Crawford died January 29, 1863, age 50 years, 12 months, 12 days, and is buried in the Blue Springs Cemetery, according to the DAR's 1934 *Vital Historical Records* compendium. Elizabeth (Harris) Crawford died intestate May 13, 1873, according to her probate/estate file. There were 15 heirs named in her unsigned and undated Last Will and Testament. *Jeptha M. Crawford was a Southern sympathizer, but had never taken up arms against the government. He had gone to the mill one day with a sack of corn to have it ground to make bread for his wife and children. He left home early in the morning and was to be back by Noon.... Three o'clock came and Elizabeth looked out and saw a company of soldiers approaching. They rode up to the door. Elizabeth saw her husband was a prisoner in their midst. Crawford was told to dismount. Then they shot him down like a wild beast before the eyes of his wife and children. Mrs. Crawford was told to get out of the house with her children, as they were going to burn the house. She asked them to let her give the little children something to eat, as they had nothing since early morning. In answer to her appeal, one of them snatched a brand from the fire and stuck it in the straw bed. Everything was soon in flames. Elizabeth Crawford hastened from the house, snatching up a few things as she went. She soon delivered her four sons (22-year-old William; twin 15-year-olds Marshall and Marion, and 13-year-old Riley) to Quantrill's camp of guerrillas and asked them to make soldiers of her sons.* See Petersen, 225-226.

Charity (McCorkle) Kerr whose husband, Nathan Barnett Kerr, rode with Quantrill was another victim of the jail collapse. Charity was the sister of guerrillas John and Jabez McCorkle. She married Nathan Kerr on January 26, 1860. Kerr was born May 1, 1841, in Kentucky. He was a farmer but became a guerrilla after Federal troops hanged his father, Moses Kerr, for being a Southern sympathizer.

On August 14, 1863, the day following the murders, Susan (Crawford) Vandevere, Armenia (Crawford) Selvey and Charity (McCorkle) Kerr were placed in crude wooden coffins and carried by ox cart back to the Lost Township and buried together in the same grave in the *Davis-Smith Cemetery*.

In this small cemetery, in the heart of a country that had seen the most vicious fighting for the past two years, they buried the bodies of the victims. It was also the burial ground for fallen comrades over whom the guerrillas had wept just a few days before. Now, the guerrillas stood side-by-side with their friends from Brooking Township as they buried the young girls who had been murdered in the most cowardly manner of the War.

Quantrill's Raid on Lawrence

The premeditated murder of these young female relatives of Quantrill's men is what many claim to have been the catalyst for Quantrill's August 21, 1863, raid on Lawrence, Kansas, though the attack by so many raiders could not have coalesced in one week; it had to have been planned for some time in advance.

Despite feeling a sense of a just retaliation in the raid on Lawrence, Southern sympathizers had little time to rejoice. An edict from General Ewing swept the country clean of citizens under martial law. His infamous "Order No. 11," forced everyone living in Jackson, Cass, Bates and northern Vernon County, except for designated towns, cities and military posts in Jackson and Cass Counties, from their homes regardless if they were loyal to the

49

Union or otherwise. One local man, Zion Flanery, who after fleeing his home during Ewing's order returned to his farm under the cover of darkness to gather in crops. He was discovered by Union soldiers and murdered while attempting to gather food for his family. The effects of the Civil War affected everyone. Anyone with Southern sympathies were driven from their homes many seeking solace with family members in other counties or states. Some headed back to their native states in the South. Many took whatever belongings they had left and headed to Texas and the safety behind Southern lines. Over 1,500 Missouri families resettled in Texas during the war.

Families from the Lost Township were forced to pack up household articles and belongings on very short notice. Small livestock were loaded on wagons. Milk cows were tied to the tailgates. The women were forced to take care of themselves and their children since their husbands and sons were in distant Confederate camps. One local resident recounted, *"It was the most terrible drive ever experience by women and children. Everybody in the county was moving at the same time. The weather was dry, hot and dusty. Dust was so thick on the fence posts, handfuls could be gathered up. Exhaustion overtook us. We usually stopped at the side of the road and bunked on the ground."*

Jabez McCorkle, Jr.

Jabez McCorkle, son of Jabez and Nancy (Fristoe) McCorkle, was 19-years-old at the start of the Civil War.[28] His brother, John McCorkle, was 20. Jabez worked as a farmhand on his uncle John Fristoe's farm just a short distance east of the Lost

---

[28] His father, Jabez/Jarvis McCorkle, Sr., was born in Christian County, Kentucky, to Lydia McCorkle in 1806. He married Nancy Fristoe October 19, 1826, at the home of his brother, Alexander McCorkle, in Clay County, Missouri. Alexander had been appointed as a guardian of Nancy Fristoe and John L. Fristoe on June 26 of that year after their father, Daniel Fristoe, died (per Clay County Wills). The Jabez/Jarvis McCorkle, Sr., family was listed in the 1850 U.S. Census in Cass County, Missouri.

Township. John McCorkle later wrote, *"I fully intended when I started to raise a crop with my Uncle John Fristoe to remain a quiet, law abiding citizen."*[29]

In the spring of 1861, when Governor Claiborne Jackson issued a call for all young men to defend the state against from what he considered to be Northern aggression, Jabez joined the Missouri State Guards with his brother, John. They were in the Battle of Lexington on September 12, 1861, but afterwards taken prisoners.

John McCorkle (left) lost a sister when the Union Jail collapsed. He and Thomas Harris, both members of Quantrill's band, posed for this picture in 1864.

The brothers tried to return to farming and put the war behind them but Union authorities demanded that they post a $5,000 bond as a guarantee they would not take up arms again against the North. While they were tending to their farms Federal patrols seized them using them as human shields while searching for bushwhackers in the hills surrounding their home. Not satisfied with that, the Federals threatened to imprison their female cousin, Mollie Wigginton, if they did not enlist in the Union army. Instead, they decided to join William Clarke Quantrill and his partisan ranger company with John McCorkle becoming his chief of scouts. John was in every major battle and skirmish involving Quantrill's guerrillas. Both John and Jabez took part in the First Battle of Independence on August 11, 1862. Sometime in late May

---

[29] Petersen, 128.

1863, as Jabez was leading a squad of guerrillas along the southern end of the valley of the Little Blue he dropped his rifle, the bullet striking him in the leg just below the right knee. He was hidden in a cave near his home and secretly cared for by his wife, Nannie, and her family. He suffered from his wound for three weeks before dying on June 2. His family and comrades carried his body up the hill and quietly buried him in the *Davis-Smith Cemetery*. In a matter of weeks, his sister, Charity (McCorkle) Kerr, would be laid to rest beside him.

Nancy "Nannie" Elizabeth Ellen (Harris) McCorkle Lilley & James E. Lilley
(granddaughter of Reuben Harris, Sr.)

Nancy (Nannie) Elizabeth Ellen Harris was born April 4, 1844. *Imagine the strife she endured in just six month's time in 1863.* She married Jabez McCorkle on March 26. He died on June 2. The family's gristmill was burned and Nannie, on her way to buy flour in Kasnas City, was arrested in July. She survived the Union jail collapse of August 13 with a broken ankle. Escaping with her life in that tragedy, she lived with her parents when Federals burned their home and gristmill around September 6. She finally left the turmoil in Jackson County and walked—*on her ailing ankle*—more than 100 miles to Howard County, Missouri.

After the War, Nannie married James E. Lilley, the son of Kentucky native, John Lilley,[30] and another of Quantrill's guerrillas. The couple was listed in the 1870 U.S. Census living in the Lee's Summit, Missouri, area. James Lilley was 33 and Nannie was reported to be 28 (actually 26). [31]

Still suffering from injuries sustained in the Union jail collapse, Nannie passed away on November 10, 1872. Only 28-years-old, she left three small children, the youngest barely three-years-old. Her husband died just a few years later on March 9, 1875. Nannie and her two husbands are buried side-by-side in the *Davis-Smith Cemetery*.

Graves of the Unknown Civil War Soldiers

Because of hard times there continued to be burials in the *Davis-Smith Cemetery* during the course of the war. Postwar research has determined that there are at least 12 to 15 unidentified Civil War soldiers buried in a circular grave. The preponderance of evidence would suggest they were all Southern men.

At the end of the war some folks returned to their homes while many remained in Texas or some other more friendly states never to return. Unfortunately the years following the war brought little respite. After Lincoln's death the reconstruction policies of the radical Republicans in Congress continued to wage harsh treatment on their former enemies. High taxes forced many to lose their farms. Where once was found large stately plantations now there was little more than overgrown prairie. The only thing that remained were blackened chimneys, stark reminders of once stately mansions

---

[30] The spelling of the surname (Lily, Lilly, Lillie, Lilley) varies between record sources. John Lilly probate/estate file dated October 1845 list, among other heirs, one James E. Lilly.

[31] James Lilly appears in the 1850 U.S. Census, age 12; E. J. Lilly, 22, appears in the 1860 U.S. Census; and, James Lillie, 33, appears in the 1870 U.S. Census.

brought to ruins from raids by Kansas Jayhawkers. Every vestige of life had been carried away.

The few brave settlers who remained along the border strived to carry on with their shattered lives. The men of the Lost Township re-plowed the ground, planted new crops and established new orchards, and constructed new homes to replace those lost during the war.

After the Civil War, one of Quantrill's men recalled: "You who were not there can not realize for a moment the dreadful passions that were roused in the hearts of men during those fearful years. The Missouri border during the war was the scene of the greatest savagery in American history. Never before or since have Americans exhibited such brutality toward fellow Americans."[32]

Preserving a Pioneer Cemetery with a Rich History

The on-site investigation compiled by the DAR reported that only one marker was left standing in the *Davis-Smith Cemetery* in 1933, that of Sarah "Sally" Ann (Davis) Landers, wife of James Landers, who died on June 14, 1851. It is now in the possession and safekeeping of Jackson County Parks and Recreation.

One hundred years ago there were no public cemeteries. Like those elsewhere the settlers of the Lost Township had

Sally Landers tombstone preserved by Jackson County

---

[32] Petersen, xvi.

family burying grounds. If a traveler carved the dead man's name on a stone to mark his grave, the next camper might rudely appropriate that stone to make his camp fireplace or to block a wagon wheel. So if the elements hadn't worn off the inscription, you could never tell the true location of a grave by where the stone might rest. Thus it was with the *Davis-Smith Cemetery*. Graves that once had field stones or wooden markers denoting the name and date of death eventually became overgrown in a tangle of weeds and brush. Irregular field stones that had presumably marked graves became unrecognizable through the years, worn down by wind and weather, or removed by insensitive farmers.

Immediately after the Civil War much of the property in the Lost Township began to change hands as the old settlers started dying off and many former Confederates moved to more friendly environs. One hundred years after the last burial in the *Davis-Smith Cemetery* very few descendants to the original land owners could be found still living in the county. In time the harsh Missouri winters, neglect and apparent vandalism played havoc with what tombstones remained in the cemetery. Stones were overturned, broken and stolen. Markers became badly eroded while others were chipped and scarred even while those who were laid to rest there continued to receive the respect of relatives and neighbors.

With the passing of time even many of the descendants had passed away, married and moved on to newer horizons and fields of endeavor. Population growth in the Lost Township reduced the once large, sometimes stately plantations, to smaller parcels as industrialization turned many who once relied on farming to more

---

SALLY

WIFE OF

JAS. LANDERS

DIED

June 14, 1851

Aged 30 yrs.

3 mos. 24 ds.

Remember friends, as you pass by,
As you are now, so once was I.
As I am now, so you shall be,
Prepare for death and follow me.

lucrative occupations. The inevitable push toward urbanization dotted the open lands around the cemetery with housing developments. The area had grown considerably and the newly built State Highway 50, running from Kansas City through Raytown to Sedalia, Missouri, coursed its way on both sides of the cemetery.

By 1987, the property surrounding the *Davis-Smith Cemetery* had been zoned commercial and the landowners who lived there at that time considered selling the 40-acre plot. A local contractor took out an option to purchase the plat and was informed at that time that a graveyard existed on the property, and one gravestone could plainly be seen next to a tree behind the owner's home (this was the aforementioned Landers tombstone). On October 5, 1989, the ownership of the property transferred to Mr. and Mrs. Everett W. and Della J. Dulaney. The Warranty Deed continued to carry—as it had for more than 100 years—an exception for the ¼-acre *Davis-Smith Cemetery.*[33] On November 16, 2006, Show-Me 350 Westridge, LLC, of Chesterfield, Missouri, acquired the deed.[34] As of this printing, the property is understood to be in foreclosure.

---

[33] Jackson County Recorder of Deeds, Document ID I1960P1033.
[34] Jackson County Recorder of Deeds, Document ID 2006E0124982.

Herbert and Dorothy Hussey owned this parcel and home once located at 12017 East 350 Highway. These ca. 1959 aerial photographs of their former homestead pinpoint the location of the *Davis-Smith Cemetery*.

There are Missouri State Cemetery Statutes that protect cemeteries and burial grounds, and there have been many suggestions on the best way to save this historical site without compromising the law.

The ¼-acre parcel is demarcated on the Jackson County tax rolls as exempt from taxes for cemetery purposes.

An *Archaeological Survey of Missouri* was completed for the site on November 1, 1995, and submitted to the Missouri Archaeological Society (ASM #23JA502; now housed at the Missouri Department of Natural Resources), identifying structures and cultural identifiers.

Interested parties and descendants of the deceased buried in the *Davis-Smith Cemetery* desire to work within the law, and in collaboration with any present landowner enveloping the *Davis-Smith Cemetery*, so that this ¼-acre plot may be located, saved, marked, and incorporated as a unique amenity to future development.

To locate the cemetery beyond "diving" or "witching," two more scientific approaches include 1) ground penetrating radar, and 2) conducting a test transect across the cemetery location by removing the "A" horizon (topsoil, 8-10" inches or so), so that a trained archaeologist could detect grave fill (as it would contrast with the surrounding un-disturbed soil).

In order to save the *Davis-Smith Cemetery*, it *might* be feasible to have the State condemn the ¼-acre parcel and have the property deeded to a living heir that still expresses interest in preserving the property, and to find and mark the existing burial pits. Numerous descendants still exist and are still very interested in the preservation of the cemetery where their ancestor's remains rest in peace.

The history of this site is inestimable, as we hope you may see from the preceding text. Most agree that the first step in order to preserve this cemetery so that future generations may have access to it is to have the ¼-acre parcel permanently marked. In addition to respecting this space for those buried there, and providing for their descendants to pay homage, permanent identification of this cemetery might make an attraction for local businesses to promote. Residents, historians and tourists interested in historical topics— from the American Revolutionary War and its veterans, to slavery, the westward trails, the tumultuous Border War and Civil War where martial law was brutally enforced, and even the connections to pioneer Daniel Boone— would appreciate the opportunity to stand over the space where these stalwart pioneers rest.

As an example, the Missouri Civil War Heritage Foundation is eagerly looking forward to having this cemetery recognized as an important site for the Civil War Sesquicentennial (150th Anniversary). And, a roadside marker designating it as a stop on the Missouri Civil War driving tour would naturally enhance tourism in the local community.

Incorporating As an Amenity to Development

At least one nearby model exists to exemplify how the *Davis-Smith Cemetery* 'might' be saved, and to allow future development to join with it into an evolving cultural landscape. In Lee's Summit, the pioneer Howard Cemetery was in the middle of a field that was eventually developed into a shopping center. The Howard Cemetery was saved, and is now part of the ambiance and historic luster of the shopping center on Woods Chapel Road.

The positive impact of the *Davis-Smith Cemetery* on state and local economies might be noticeable, and could be used as a model for similar developments in any community across our country. *The Davis-Smith Cemetery is, indeed, one of America's treasures.*

But, most of all, preserving the *Davis-Smith Cemetery* is a chance to honor those who sacrificed for us, by guaranteeing the way of life we enjoy today.

SELECTED BIBLIOGRAPHY

Throughout the years the *Davis-Smith Cemetery* retained its notoriety being mentioned in numerous historical files, records and books. Names and dates of the deceased remained well known and published in public records. In addition to the sources outlined above, the *Davis-Smith Cemetery* and/or the people buried there, are mentioned in the following:

Bonnewitz, Roberta L., and Nancy L. Ferguson. *Index, Names Found in Oregon Donation Land Claims with Missouri Connections Abstracted from Genealogical Material in Oregon Land Claims, Volumes I and II, as Abstracted by members of the Genealogical Forum of Portland.* (Raytown, Mo.: Roberta L. Bonnewitz, 1991).

Bonnewitz, Roberta Leinweber. The *Lost Township, Jackson County, Missouri, Township 48, Range 32 West.* (Raytown, Mo: Roberta L. Bonnewitz, 2009).

Bonnewitz, Roberta L., and Lois T. Allen. *Raytown Remembers: The Story of a Santa Fe Trail Town* (Raytown, Mo: Roberta L. Bonnewitz & Lois T. Allen, 1975).

Daughters of the American Revolution, Kansas City Chapter. *Vital Historical Records, Jackson County, Missouri: 1826-1876.* Reprint of 1934 original, with a new, full-name index compiled by David W. Jackson and Suzanne Vinduska. (Independence, Mo.: Jackson County Historical Society, 2009).

Findlen, Rose Ann. *Missouri Star: The Life and Times of Martha A. "Mattie" (Livingston) Lykins Bingham*. (Independence, Mo.: Jackson County Historical Society, 2011).

Hale, Donald R. *They Called Him Bloody Bill*. (Independence, Mo.: Two Trails Publishing, 1975).

Hale, Donald R. and Joanne Eakin. *Branded as Rebels*. (Independence, Mo.: Two Trails Publishing, 1994).

Harris, Charles F. "Catalyst for Terror: The Collapse of the Women's Prison in Kansas City." *Missouri Historical Review* 1995 (April), 290-306.

Jackson County Assessment Department, Independence, Missouri.

Jackson County Genealogical Society. *Jackson County, Missouri, Deeds, 1827-1845*. Volume I. (Independence, Mo.: Jackson County Genealogical Society, 2001).

Jackson County Genealogical Society. *Jackson County, Missouri, Deeds, 1845-1851*. Volume II. (Independence, Mo.: Jackson County Genealogical Society, 2003).

Jackson County Recorder of Deeds, Independence, Missouri.

Jackson, David W. *Conserving Missouri Cemeteries*. (Independence, Mo.: Jackson County Historical Society, 2008).

Meador, Victor. *Jackson County, Missouri, Marriages, 1828-1862*. (Independence, Mo.: Jackson County Genealogical Society, 1997).

Meador, Victor. *Jackson County, Missouri, Wills and Administrations, 1828-1862*. (Independence, Mo.: Jackson County Genealogical Society, 1997).

Petersen, Paul R. *Quantrill of Missouri: The Making of a Warrior: the man, The Myth, the Soldier.* (Nashville, Tn: Cumberland House, 2003).

Petersen, Paul R. *Quantrill at Lawrence.* (Gretna, La.: Pelican Publishing Co., 2011).

Poppino, Hattie, E. Population Schedules, Bureau of the Census, Jackson County, Mo., 1830 and 1840: Fifth Federal Census, first taken in Missouri. (Kansas City, Mo.: Hattie E. Poppino, 1956).

Poppino, Hattie, E. *Index to U.S. Census Schedules, Jackson County, Missouri, 1850.* (Kansas City, Mo.: Hattie E. Poppino, 1959).

Poppino, Hattie, E. *Index to U.S. Census Schedules, Jackson County, Missouri, 1860.* (Kansas City, Mo.: Hattie E. Poppino, 1964).

Poppino, Hattie, E. *Index to U.S. Census Schedules, Jackson County, Missouri, 1870.* (Kansas City, Mo.: Hattie E. Poppino, 1970).

Union Historical Company. *History of Jackson County, Missouri.* Reprint of 1881 original, with new index compiled by Felix Eugene Snider. (Cape Girardeau, Mo.: Ramfre Press, 1966).

Wilcox, Pearl. *Jackson County Pioneers.* Reprint of 1975 original. (Independence, Mo.: Jackson County Historical Society, 1991).

ILLUSTRATIONS

14. Map from the *Illustrated Historical Atlas of Jackson County, Missouri*. Reprint of 1877 original. (Independence, Mo.: Jackson County Historical Society, 2007).

16. The south-facing, front façade of the 1838 Jackson County Courthouse on Independence Square, ca. 1850. Courtesy of Jackson County Historical Society, JCHS004862L.

18. The log cabin of Revolutionary War veteran, William Moore, on Ess Road at Little Blue, Missouri (today, Kansas City), typical of an 1820s Jackson County home like that of Lewis Starr. Courtesy of Jackson County Historical Society, JCHS007347CM.

25. Valley of the Little Blue River. Courtesy of Paul R. Petersen private collection.

28. 1859 West Fork of the Little Blue Baptist Church. Courtesy of Paul Petersen private collection.

38. John T. House and family, ca. 1881. As taken from the *History of Jackson County, Missouri*. (Kansas City, Mo.: Union Publishing Company, 1881).

40. Daniel Boone Scholl. Courtesy of Emory Cantey as viewed at http://www.quantrillsguerrillas.com.

47. Nancy "Nannie" Elizabeth Ellen (Harris) McCorkle (later Lilley) and Charity (McCorkle) Kerr. Courtesy of Jackson County Historical Society, Quantrill Society Collection of Donald R. Hale, JCHS006174M.

51. John McCorkle (left) lost a sister when the Union Jail collapsed. He and Thomas B. Harris, both members of Quantrill's band, posed for this picture in 1864. Courtesy of Jackson County Historical Society, Quantrill Society Collection of Donald R. Hale, JCHS005496S.

52. Nancy "Nannie" Ellen (Harris) McCorkle Lilley and James Lilley, after the Civil War. Courtesy of Jackson County Historical Society, Quantrill Society Collection of Donald R. Hale, JCHS006182M.

54. Tombstone of Sarah "Sally" Ann (Davis) Landers. Courtesy of John K. Peterson, Curator, Jackson County Parks and Recreation Department.

57. Two aerials views of the Hussey homestead, Kansas City, Missouri, showing the location of the *Davis-Smith Cemetery* and other landmarks inscribed by Sue Frank. Courtesy of Jackson County Historical Society, gift of Mrs. Dorothy Hussey, JCHS007346AM and JCHS007346BM.

APPENDIX

Missouri Cemetery Statutes

For the edification of Missouri residents trying to protect sacred burial spaces in their communities, the State of Missouri provides:

Missouri Revised Statutes
Chapter 214
Sections Section 214.131; Section 214.385; and, 214.455

Every person who shall knowingly destroy, mutilate, disfigure, deface, injure or remove any tomb, monument or gravestone, or other structure placed in any abandoned family cemetery or private burying ground, or any fence, railing, or other work for the protection or ornamentation of any such cemetery or place of burial of any human being, or tomb, monument or gravestone, memento, or memorial, or other structure aforesaid, or of any lot within such cemetery is guilty of a class A misdemeanor.

For the purposes of this section and subsection 1 of section 214.132, an "abandoned family cemetery" or "private burying ground" shall include those cemeteries or burying grounds which have not been deeded to the public as provided in chapter 214, and in which no body has been interred for at least twenty-five years.

If the operator of any cemetery or another authorized person moves a grave marker, memorial or monument in the cemetery for any reason, the operator or other authorized person shall replace the grave marker, memorial or monument to its original position within a reasonable time.

INDEX

ABOUT THE AUTHORS

Paul R. Petersen is an award-winning author and educator who lectures on the Missouri-Kansas Border War. A highly decorated retired master sergeant with the United States Marine Corps, Petersen is an infantry combat veteran of Vietnam, Desert Storm and Iraqi Freedom.

His combat experience brings insight into the character of William Clarke Quantrill, the man who was responsible for developing modern guerrilla warfare.

Author of three books, *Quantrill of Missouri*, *Quantrill in Texas* and *Quantrill at Lawrence*, Petersen's insights brings complex patterns of events into clear focus, identifies the personalities involved along the border and quotes memorably from firsthand accounts giving a clear understanding of the temper of the times. *Quantrill at Lawrence* is the only account explaining the causes, reasoning and justification for the 1863 Lawrence raid. It is the first time a complete story has been written using accounts by both the victims and the raiders. Researched facts that earlier historians have intentionally omitted have been included.

Quantrill of Missouri received the distinguished Perry Award for Best Book in 2004 and *Quantrill in Texas* received the 2009 Milton F. Perry Best Non-Fiction Award.

David W. Jackson received a BS magna cum laude in historic preservation, archives studies from Southeast Missouri State University.

He is the founder and director of The Orderly Pack Rat [orderlypackrat.com], publisher of Jackson's first book, *Direct Your Letters to San Jose: The California Gold Rush Letters of James and David Lee Campbell, 1849–1852* (2000); subsequent, *Recipes of Our Past: Morsels from Our Grandmothers' Recipe Boxes* (2005; 2011); and, forthcoming *A Family Secret Unshackled: Arthur Jackson's Birth into Slavery* [tentative title].

Since 2000, Jackson, as director of Archives and Education for the Jackson County Historical Society, has served as editor and contributed to the nonprofit organization's scholarly JOURNAL; administers all of its Archives operations; services thousands of patron requests annually through its Research Library; manages its physical and virtual bookshop; updates its website; coordinates an archival internship and volunteer program; presents on behalf of its Speakers' Bureau; contributes regular, local history-related articles to area newspapers; and has written and/or directed the publishing of several articles, booklets, pamphlets, and books through the Society's imprint.

Jackson's other full-length books include: *LOCK DOWN: Outlaws, Lawmen and Frontier Justice in Jackson County, Missouri* (Independence, Mo.: Jackson County Historical Society, 2009); and, *Kansas City Chronicles: An Up-to-Date History* (Charleston, Sc.: The History Press, 2010).

www.ingramcontent.com/pod-product-compliance
Lightning Source LLC
Chambersburg PA
CBHW060144050426
42448CB00010B/2283